D Helps

Best Damn Interview Guide Ever:
How Can an Eskimo Ice the Interview?

Best Damn Interview Guide Ever

"Preparation is the key to success. It's the difference between hoping to get the job and knowing you're going to get the job."
Derek Phelps, Recruiter and Headhunter

D Helps
Why Write This?

As a seasoned recruiter and headhunter with over a decade of experience, I have had the privilege of interviewing thousands of applicants for positions across various industries, including manufacturing, finance, engineering, sales, accounting, and customer service. My expertise spans the entire organizational spectrum, from C-suite executives to production line staff, and from top talent to administrative assistants.

Throughout my career, I've worked closely with both candidates and employers to identify the perfect match for each role. I've witnessed firsthand the triumphs of top performers and the pitfalls of those who faltered. I've seen what sets exceptional candidates apart and what mistakes can make or break an interview.

The Value of Preparation

I passionately believe that the time spent preparing for an interview is invaluable. It's a chance to polish your skills, refine your message, and showcase your personality. When you walk into an interview room, you want to be confident that you've done everything possible to present yourself in the best light. That's why I'm committed to sharing my expertise with you.

Aiming for Success

This guide is designed to help you navigate the complex world of job interviews with ease. Whether you're a seasoned professional or just starting out, my goal is to equip you with the tools and strategies necessary to succeed. From crafting a compelling elevator pitch to acing behavioral questions, I'll guide you through the entire interview process.

Lessons from the Front Lines

Throughout these pages, I'll share real-life stories of candidates who nailed their interviews and those who didn't. You'll learn from their successes and mistakes, gaining valuable insights into what works and what doesn't. My aim is to provide you with a comprehensive guide that will help you stand out from the competition and land your dream job.

Get Ready to Shine

So, if you're ready to take your interview skills to the next level, let's get started! With my expert guidance, you'll be well on your way to acing your next interview and launching your career to new heights. Thanks job seeker let's get started.
D Helps

Table of Contents

1. Introduction..8
   - Overview of the Guide
   - Importance of Preparation
   - How to Use This Guide

2. Understanding the Interview Process......................9
   - The Psychology of the Interview
   - First Impressions Matter: Dressing for Success
   - Body Language and Nonverbal Cues
   - Building Rapport: Connecting with the Interviewer

3. Mastering the Basics.....................................17
   - Understanding the Job Application Process
   - The Numbers Game
   - Working with Recruiters: A Word of Caution
   - Crafting Your Elevator Pitch
   - Tailoring Your Resume and Cover Letter
   - Preparing for Common Interview Questions

4. Acing the Interview......................................25
   - Tips for Virtual Interviews
   - Handling Difficult Questions with Grace
   - The Power of Silence
   - Closing the Interview Strong

5. The Secrets to Success...................................32

- The Art of the Thank-You Note
- Following Up Effectively
- Building Relationships After the Interview

6. The Negotiation Process……………………………….39
    - Understanding Your Worth
    - Negotiating Salary and Benefits
    - The Art of Compromise

7. Common Interview Mistakes to Avoid……………42
    - Overcoming Interview Anxiety
    - The Importance of a Positive Attitude

8. Advanced Interview Technique…………………...…44
    - Behavioral Interviewing: A Deep Dive
    - The STAR Method: A Framework for Effective Storytelling
    - Case Interview Strategies
    - Group Interview Tips

9. Exceptional Answers to Common Interview Questions..46
    - Top Interview Questions
    - Behavioral Interview Questions
    - Technical Interview Questions
    - Situational Interview Questions
    - General Interview Questions

10. Questions You Should Ask………………..……….49
    - About the Role and Team
    - Company Culture and Values

- Challenges and Opportunities

11. Professionalism in the Interview...........................51
    - The Importance of Professionalism
    - Maintaining a Comfortable Yet Professional Demeanor
    - Tips for Virtual Interviews
    - Dos and Don'ts of Interview Etiquette

12. The Close..53
    - How to Express Your Interest in the Job
    - The Power of Asking for the Position
    - Follow-Up Strategies

13. Follow-Up and Networking................................55
    - Sending a Thank-You Note
    - Building Your Network
    - Leveraging LinkedIn and Other Professional Platforms

14. Conclusion..57
    - Recap of Key Takeaways
    - Final Encouragement
    - Resources for Further Reading

Chapter 1: Introduction

"Best Damn Interview Questions Ever" is designed to equip you with the tools and strategies necessary to excel in your next job interview. Whether you are a recent graduate or a seasoned professional, this guide will help you stand out and land your dream job.

Preparation is crucial for a successful interview. This guide covers everything from understanding the interview process to crafting exceptional answers to frequent questions. By the end of this guide, you will be well-prepared to navigate any interview with confidence.

Use this guide as a comprehensive resource. Each chapter builds on the earlier one, providing a step-by-step approach to mastering the interview process. Feel free to reference specific chapters as needed.

Chapter 2: Understanding the Interview Process

The Psychology of the Interview

Understanding the psychology behind the interview process can give you a significant advantage. Interviewers seek candidates who are confident, prepared, and a good fit for the company culture. By understanding their perspective, you can tailor your responses to meet their expectations.

First Impressions Matter: Dressing for Success

First impressions are crucial in the interview process. How you present yourself visually can significantly affect an interviewer's feeling of you before you even say a word. Dressing appropriately for the interview not only shows respect for the process and the company but also shows your professionalism and attention to detail.

Why Appearance Matters

- **Professional Image:** Your attire reflects your understanding of the company culture and the position you're applying for.

- **Confidence Boost**: When you look good, you feel good. Dressing well can boost your confidence and help you perform better in the interview.

- **Respect: Proper dress** shows that you take the opportunity seriously and respect the interviewer's time.

"When I send out candidates, I have a checklist where I always ask, 'What are you going to wear?' Generally, I'm shocked when candidates really haven't thought about it beforehand. Second visits may be on a plant floor. Sometimes these locations are quite hot and require the right shoes. Think about the environment."

By considering the interview environment and being prepared to adjust accordingly, candidates can make a strong, professional impression throughout the entire process. Let me emphasize, "It's not just about dressing for success – it's about dressing for the specific situation you'll be in."

Tips for Dressing for Success

1. **Research the Company** Culture: Different industries and companies have varying dress codes. Research the company to understand their typical attire.

2. **Err on the Side of Conservative**: When in doubt, it's better to be slightly overdressed than underdressed.

3. **Choose Appropriate Colors**: Stick to neutral colors like navy, gray, or black for suits. Avoid overly bright or distracting colors.

4. **Ensure Your Clothes Fit Well:** Ill-fitting clothes can be distracting and unprofessional. Make sure your outfit is comfortable and fits properly.

5. **Pay Attention to Details**: Polish your shoes, ensure your clothes are wrinkle-free, and check for any loose threads or missing buttons.

6. **Minimal Accessories**: Keep jewelry and accessories simple and professional. Avoid anything too flashy or noisy.

7. **Grooming:** Ensure your hair is neat and styled conservatively. For those who wear makeup, keep it natural and professional.

8. **Prepare the Night Before**: Lay out your outfit the night before to avoid last-minute stress or wardrobe malfunctions.

Industry-Specific Considerations

- **Corporate/Finance:** Traditional business attire is usually expected. A suit in a conservative color is typically right.

- **Creative Industries:** While still professional, there may be more flexibility. Business casual might be acceptable, but always err on the side of more formal.
- **Tech Startups:** Often have a more casual dress code, but for an interview, business casual is usually a safe bet.

Remember, your goal is to make your qualifications and personality stand out, not your outfit. By dressing appropriately, you ensure that the focus stays on your skills and what you can bring to the role.

A Final Note

As Derek Phelps, your friendly headhunter, always says: "Dress for the job you want, not the job you have. When you walk into that interview room, you want the interviewer to be able to envision you in the role from the moment they see you."

Body Language and Nonverbal Cues

Nonverbal cues can speak volumes about your confidence, preparedness, and overall suitability for a job. Effective use of body language can enhance your interview performance and create a positive impression on the interviewer. Here are some key tips to help you master nonverbal communication during your interview:

The Importance of Body Language

Body language is a crucial part of communication. It can reinforce your words or contradict them, affecting how the interviewer perceives you. Nonverbal cues can show confidence, enthusiasm, and attentiveness—all qualities that employers value.

Tips for Effective Body Language

1. **Maintain Eye Contact:**

- Eye contact is a powerful way to show confidence and engagement. Maintain steady but not overly intense eye contact with the interviewer.

- Avoid looking away too often, as it can make you appear disinterested or untrustworthy.

2. **Posture:**

    - Sit or stand with good posture. Keep your back straight and your shoulders relaxed.

    - Leaning slightly forward can show interest and engagement but avoid slouching or appearing too casual.

3. **Gestures:**

    - Use open gestures to emphasize your points. Keep your hands visible and avoid crossing your arms, which can make you appear closed off.

    - Be mindful of your hand movements. Use them sparingly and purposefully to avoid appearing nervous or distracted.

4. **Facial Expressions:**

    - Smile appropriately to convey warmth and enthusiasm. A genuine smile can help you build rapport with the interviewer.

    - Avoid frowning or displaying negative facial expressions, as they can detract from your message.

5. **Active Listening:**

    - Nod occasionally to show that you are following the conversation.

- Lean slightly forward when the interviewer is speaking to show interest and engagement.

Avoiding Common Pitfalls

1. **Fidgeting:**
   - Avoid fidgeting with your hands, hair, or objects. This can make you appear nervous or disinterested.
   - If you tend to fidget, try to keep your hands still by holding a pen or placing them on your lap.

2. **Crossing Your Arms or Legs:**
   - Crossing your arms can make you appear defensive or closed off. Try to keep your arms at your sides or rest them on the table.
   - Crossing your legs can also give off a negative impression. Keep your feet flat on the floor or cross your ankles instead.

3. **Slouching:**
   - Slouching can make you appear bored or disinterested. Maintain good posture throughout the interview.
   - If you find yourself slouching, take a deep breath and straighten your back.

Putting It All Together

Effective body language is about balance and authenticity. Aim to come across as confident and engaged, but also genuine and approachable. Practice your nonverbal communication skills before the interview by role-playing with a friend or recording yourself to find areas for improvement.

Final Thoughts

Mastering nonverbal cues can significantly enhance your interview performance. By keeping eye contact, using open gestures, and actively listening, you can create a positive impression on the interviewer and improve your chances of success. Remember, practice makes perfect, so take the time to refine your body language skills before your next interview.

Good luck! With the right preparation and mindset, you'll be well on your way to acing your next interview and landing your dream job.

Building Rapport: Connecting with the Interviewer

Building a connection with the interviewer is a crucial aspect of any job interview. It can set you apart from other candidates, create a positive impression, and ultimately influence the outcome of the interview. Here are some strategies to help you build rapport and establish a strong connection with your interviewer:

Research Your Interviewer

Before the interview, take the time to research your interviewer. Utilize social media platforms like LinkedIn to learn about their background, interests, and experiences. This preparation can help you find commonalities that can serve as excellent conversation starters.

Seek Commonalities

Find shared interests, experiences, or values that can form the basis of your connection. This could include attending the same college, hailing from the same region, or sharing a passion for a particular hobby or sports team. Bringing up these common interests during the early stages of the interview can help establish a rapport.

Use Nonverbal Cues

Nonverbal cues play a significant role in building rapport. Extend a firm handshake, smile warmly, and keep eye contact. These

D Helps

gestures show enthusiasm and engagement. During the interview, continue using effective nonverbal practices such as nodding to show you're listening and making eye contact to help the interviewer feel connected with you.

Be Authentic

Be genuine in your responses and avoid presenting a facade to impress the interviewer. Authenticity is clear from the depth of your answers, and it makes it easier to generate engaging conversation. Embrace your unique personality, skills, and experiences. This approach helps you connect more naturally with the interviewer.

Active Listening

Active listening is essential for building rapport. Demonstrate understanding by paraphrasing the interviewer's points and asking relevant follow-up questions. This shows that you are genuinely interested in their insights and perspectives. Engage in the conversation by asking open-ended questions that encourage the interviewer to share more about themselves or the company.

Engage in Meaningful Conversation

Use the environment to your advantage. If you're in the interviewer's office, look for personal items or decor that can spark interesting conversations. For example, if you see sports memorabilia, you can comment on it and find common ground.

Ask Personal and Relevant Questions

Ask questions that integrate the interviewer into the conversation. For instance, ask about their role in the company, their story with the organization, or what they enjoy most about working there. These questions show that you are interested in growing with the company and in the interviewer's experiences.

Avoid Controversy

Avoid controversial topics such as politics or religion. These subjects can create discomfort and may offend the interviewer. Keep the conversation light and professional, focusing on shared interests and work-related topics.

Maintain Consistency and Follow-Up

To keep rapport alive and strong, be consistent in your words and actions. Honor your commitments and follow up on your promises. After the interview, send a thank-you note or message that reiterates your interest and mentions any commonalities or interesting points discussed during the interview.

Utilize Storytelling

Use storytelling to make your responses more memorable and relatable. Describe your accomplishments, skills, and strengths in a narrative format, such as using the Situation, Action, Result (STAR) method. This approach can create an emotional connection with the interviewer and make your answers more engaging.

Conclusion

Building rapport with the interviewer is not just a nice-to-have skill; it's a crucial one for both interviewers and interviewees. By establishing a connection, you can create a positive first impression, reduce anxiety and stress, enhance communication and understanding, and foster trust and respect. Remember to be yourself, show interest in the interviewer, and engage in meaningful conversations to build a strong and lasting rapport.

By following these strategies, you can build a strong connection with your interviewer, making the interview more enjoyable and increasing your chances of success.

Chapter 3: Mastering the Basics

Understanding the Job Application Process

As you embark on your job search journey, it's essential to understand the realities of the application process. This knowledge will help you set realistic expectations and keep a positive attitude throughout your search.

The Numbers Game

On average, job seekers may need to send out 10-20 applications to secure a face-to-face interview. However, this number can vary significantly based on several factors:

- **Job Market:** A competitive job market may require more applications.

- **Industry:** Certain industries, such as tech or healthcare, may have higher competition.

- **Job Level:** Higher-level positions often receive fewer applications but require more rigorous screening processes.

- **Your Concise Resume and Cover Letter:** A well-crafted resume and cover letter can increase your chances of getting an interview.

- **Networking:** Using your network can lead to more targeted job applications.

- **Geographic Location:** Your location and the specific job market you're targeting can also influence the number of applications required.

Remember, quality over quantity is key. One well-targeted application can be more effective than ten generic ones. Focus on tailoring your resume and cover letter to each specific job, and don't be discouraged by rejections. Persistence and a positive attitude are crucial to finding your dream job.

Working with Recruiters: A Word of Caution

As a job seeker, you may find yourself working with recruiters or headhunters. While these professionals can be valuable allies in your job search, it's important to remember a few key points:

- **Professionalism is Key:** Even if you feel comfortable in a recruiter's office, keep a professional demeanor. Avoid sharing personal stories or family problems that an employer would not want to hear.

- **Recruiters Work for Employers:** Remember that recruiters are paid by employers to find the best candidates. They are not your personal job search advocates.

- **Put Your Best Foot Forward:** When interacting with recruiters, always present your best self. Be honest, professional, and highlight your skills and experiences that make you an excellent candidate.

- **Tailor Your Approach:** Just as you would with a potential employer, tailor your resume and communication to the specific roles the recruiter is trying to fill.

By understanding these aspects of the job application process, you can approach your job search with realistic expectations and a strategic mindset. Remember, the goal is to find not just any job, but the right job for you. Stay persistent, keep a positive attitude, and continue to refine your approach based on the feedback you receive.

Crafting Your Elevator Pitch

An elevator pitch is a concise and powerful summary of who you are, what you do, and what makes you the ideal candidate for the job. It's your chance to make a lasting impression on the interviewer and set yourself apart from the competition.

The Perfect "Tell Me About Yourself" Response

D Helps

Your elevator pitch should be a brief, 30-second to 1-minute overview of your professional brand when you are introducing yourself. It should answer the question, "Who am I and what value can I bring to this organization?" Keep it focused, relevant, and impactful. Avoid sharing personal hobbies or interests unless they're directly related to the job. When writing a few words can sum it up. Remember Hank Hill? He is the lead character in King of the Hill. His pitch is perfect. He proudly sells "propane and propane accessories."

Example of a Strong Elevator Pitch

Here's an example of an effective elevator pitch:

"Hi, I'm [Your Name], an initiative-taking and experienced [Your Profession] with a proven track record of [Desirable Skill or Achievement

Tailoring Your Resume and Cover Letter

A well-crafted resume and cover letter are crucial in today's competitive job market. These documents serve as the first impression of you to potential employers, and their quality can significantly impact your chances of getting an interview. In this chapter, we'll explore how to tailor your resume and cover letter to specific job openings, leveraging the power of AI tools to create professional makeovers.

Understanding the Importance of Tailoring

1. **Increased Relevance**: Tailoring your application materials to the job description and requirements increases your relevance to the position. This shows that you've taken the time to understand the employer's needs and that you have the skills and experience to meet those needs.
2. **Enhanced Visibility**: Customized resumes and cover letters are more likely to pass through applicant tracking

systems (ATS) and catch the eye of hiring managers. This is because they contain the keywords and phrases used in the job posting, making them more visible in searches.

Preparing for Common Interview Questions

Preparation is key to answering common interview questions with confidence. By understanding the most frequent questions and practicing your responses, you can present yourself effectively and highlight your qualifications. This chapter covers the most common interview questions and gives sample answers to help you prepare.

Common Interview Questions

1. **Tell Me About Yourself:**
   - Sample Answer: "I'm an experienced [Your Profession] with [Number] years of experience in [Your Field]. Throughout my career, I have developed a strong background in [Relevant Skills] and have consistently delivered results in [Specific Achievements]. In my earlier role at [Previous Company], I [Describe a Key Accomplishment]. I am passionate about [Your Interests] and am excited about the opportunity to bring my skills and experience to [Company Name]."

Typically, I will stop a candidate here after a few words. The key is not the story of your life. We don't want to come across as a politician being brought up in middle America etc. etc. I did this and this and I really love doing this. They should be skills the employer needs. You can make it more powerful with credibility such as my efforts were awarded a kudos from my boss. Then really shock them you can ask a question here and create a conversation a dialogue with the interviewer that will land that job.

2. **Why Are You Interested in This Position?**

D Helps

- Sample Answer: "I am interested in this position because it aligns perfectly with my career goals and allows me to leverage my **strengths in** [Relevant Skills]. I have always admired [Company Name]'s reputation for [Company's Strengths], and I believe that my background in [Relevant Experience] will enable me to make a significant contribution to your team."

You don't have to sound like a robot. I read a job ad from an employer that sounded compelling. Opportunity and growth and were suited to my past experiences to be effective in the role. I made the call to them to say I know we could fill it because I understood what he was looking for.

Once a recruiter I worked with was filling a difficult ask. He was looking for a doctor to fill a position in a ridiculously small and lonely town. He said it was easy once you know what really to look for. He needed a fisherman who happened to be a Physician. He found that.

3. **What Are Your Strengths and Weaknesses?**

   - Sample Answer: "One of my strengths is my ability to [Describe a Strength], which has enabled me to achieve [Specific Achievement]. Additionally, I am proficient in [Another Strength], which has been beneficial in [Relevant Situation]. As for weaknesses, I have struggled with [Describe a Weakness]. However, I am actively working on improving in this area by [Describe Steps Taken to Improve]."

A candidate gave me a weakness of not having the training completed in a particular process. He had looked up the course and picked a date for the training and had written it as a goal for the end of the year, money being a major factor. The employer was impressed with the goal, hired him and **paid for the course.**

4. **Tell Me About a Time When You Overcame a Challenge:**

- Sample Answer: "In one instance, I faced a significant challenge when [Describe the Challenge]. To overcome this, I [Describe Actions Taken]. As a result, [Describe Positive Outcome]. This experience taught me the importance of [Lesson Learned], and I have applied this knowledge to other challenges I have faced."

Raising a family or using personal experience away from the work force is tricky. Look back over your past employment situations and find a time when you learned a new way of doing or processing a situation that yielded results.

5. **How Do You Handle Conflict?**

    - Sample Answer: "When faced with conflict, I believe in resolving issues through open communication and mutual respect. For example, [Describe a Specific Conflict]. To address this, I [Describe Actions Taken]. The situation was resolved when [Describe Resolution]. This approach has helped me maintain strong relationships with colleagues and achieve positive outcomes in challenging situations."

I find many of my longest lasting relationships are with colleagues. Heck, we spend more time together than family. By listening and respecting my peers I hope to develop long term professional lasting relationships.

6. **Describe Your Leadership Style:**

    - Sample Answer: "My leadership style is [Describe Your Leadership Style, e.g., collaborative, visionary, etc.]. I believe in empowering my team members and fostering an environment of trust and mutual respect. In my previous role at [Previous Company], I [Describe a Leadership Example]. As a result, [Describe Positive Outcome]. I am committed to leading by **example and supporting my team's growth and development.**"

D Helps

I find many candidates may not have been in leadership positions they can pull out of a hat. You may have never had 20 indirect reports or 5 direct reports. possibly you trained the team in a customer service session or even coached the bowling team. Think hard of the times you trained, went first, or developed a plan. Then talk about that. Again, turn it around and ask if the role has any direct or indirect reports. Interviews are a give and take.

7. Where Do You See Yourself in Five Years?

- Sample Answer: "In five years, I envision myself [Describe Career Goal, e.g., having advanced to a leadership role, expanding my skills, etc.]. I am particularly interested in [Specific Goal or Area of Interest] and believe that this position at [Company Name] will provide me with the opportunities and challenges necessary to achieve my long-term career goals."

Only a few can pull off the "I want your job" response. Avoid that answer. Talk about your goals that are written down. They may be personal financial and professional goals just share the professional ones

Tips for Preparation

1. **Research the Company**: Understand the company's mission, values, and culture. This knowledge will help you craft your responses to align with the company's goals and values.

2. **Practice Your** Answers Rehearse your responses to frequent questions until you feel comfortable and confident.

3. **Prepare Questions for the Interviewer:** Use the interview as an opportunity to gain experience more about the company and the role. Prepare thoughtful questions that show your interest and engagement.

4. **Be Yourself:** While it's important to prepare, remember to be authentic and genuine in your responses. Show your personality and enthusiasm for the role.

5. **Stay Positive:** Keep a cheerful outlook throughout the interview. Focus on your strengths and what you can bring to the company, even when discussing challenges or weaknesses.

Remember, the interviewer wants to hire you. Their job is to find the right candidate for the position. All hires are critical and time-consuming. Once they get you onboard, they can focus on other important tasks. Help them by presenting yourself as the ideal candidate. By preparing for common interview questions and following these tips, you can build confidence and present yourself effectively in any interview situation.

Chapter 4: Acing the Interview

Tips for Virtual Interviews

The COVID-19 pandemic has led to a significant increase in virtual interviews, as remote work and social distancing measures have become the new normal. While the core principles of a successful interview remain the same, there are some unique considerations for virtual interviews. In this chapter, we'll explore tips to help you ace your next virtual interview.

Prepare Your Environment

1. **Find** a Quiet, Well-Lit Space: Choose a room with minimal background noise and distractions. Ensure the space is well-lit, with the light source positioned in front of you to avoid shadows on your face.

2. **Minimize Clutter:** Tidy up your background and remove any personal items or distractions that could be visible during the interview.

3. **Test Your Technology**: Ensure your computer, webcam, and microphone are functioning properly. Do a test run with a friend or family member to find and address any technical issues.

Present a Professional Appearance

1. **Dress the Part**: Treat a virtual interview the same as an in-person one. Wear professional attire, as you would for a traditional interview.

2. **Maintain Eye Contact**: Look directly at the camera, not the screen, to create the illusion of eye contact with the interviewer.

3. **Sit Up Straight**: Keep good posture and avoid slouching or leaning back in your chair.

Engage with the Interviewer

1. **Speak Clearly and Slowly:** Due to potential audio delays or connection issues, it's important to speak clearly and at a moderate pace.

2. **Use Nonverbal Cues:** Nod, smile, and use hand gestures to show engagement and interest, just as you would in an in-person interview.

3. **Minimize Distractions:** Close any unnecessary tabs or applications on your computer to avoid potential distractions.

Troubleshoot Technical Issues

1. **Have a Backup Plan:** Find a backup location or device in case of technical difficulties during the interview.

2. **Communicate Proactively:** If you experience any technical issues, inform the interviewer at once and work together to find a solution.

3. **Remain Calm:** Keep a professional demeanor even if you meet technical problems. The interviewer will appreciate your ability to stay composed.

Follow Up Effectively

1. **Send a Thank-You Note**: After the interview, send a follow-up email to express your gratitude and reiterate your interest in the position.

2. **Provide Feedback**: If you have any suggestions for improving the virtual interview process, consider sharing them with the employer.

Remember, while the format may be different, the goal of a virtual interview stays the same: to highlight your qualifications, job fit, and enthusiasm for the role. By following these tips, you can navigate the virtual landscape and present your best self to potential employers.

Handling Difficult Questions with Grace

D Helps

Managing tough questions with confidence can set you apart from other candidates. Learn strategies for responding to challenging questions without getting flustered. A simple technique is to pause before answering, using phrases like "That's a good question" or "Well, in the situation you discussed, I would do..."

The Power of Silence

In the high-stakes environment of a job interview, silence can be a surprisingly powerful tool. Knowing when to use silence and how to navigate awkward pauses can set you apart from other candidates and show your poise and confidence.

The Benefits of Silence

1. **Allows for Reflection:** Silence gives you the opportunity to pause, gather your thoughts, and formulate a thoughtful response.

2. **Creates Emphasis:** Strategically placed silences can help emphasize important points and make your responses more impactful.

3. **Showcases Confidence:** Sitting comfortably in silence, rather than rushing to fill the void, conveys self-assurance and composure.

4. **Helps the Interviewer Process Information**: Silence gives the interviewer time to fully absorb and consider your earlier statements.

When to Use Silence

1. **After a Question**: Take a brief pause after the interviewer asks a question to ensure you fully understand it before responding.

2. **During Your Response:** Use short pauses to emphasize key points or allow the interviewer to interject with a follow-up question.

3. **Before Providing an Example:** Pause before sharing a specific example or story to build anticipation and focus the interviewer's attention.

4. **When Reflecting on a Question:** If you need time to gather your thoughts, take a moment of silence to collect your ideas before answering.

Avoiding Filler Words

Many people instinctively try to fill silences with filler words like "um," "uh," or "you know." While this is a common habit, it can undermine your confidence and professionalism. Instead, practice using silence intentionally, without feeling the need to constantly speak.

Strategies for Navigating Awkward Pauses

1. **Breathe and Relax**: If you find yourself in an unexpected silence, take a deep breath to keep your composure.

2. **Reframe the Pause**: Rather than viewing it as an awkward moment, reframe the silence as an opportunity to thoughtfully consider your response.

3. **Ask a Clarifying Question**: If you're unsure why the interviewer has paused, politely ask a clarifying question to better understand their intent.

4. **Avoid Rambling:** Resist the urge to fill the silence with unnecessary information. Stick to concise, well-thought-out responses.

Mastering the Art of Silence

Incorporating strategic silence into your interview technique takes practice, but the rewards can be significant. By learning **to** use silence effectively, you can show your confidence, critical thinking skills, and ability to communicate effectively under pressure.

Remember, silence is a powerful tool in your interview arsenal. Use it wisely to enhance your performance and leave a lasting impression on the interviewer.

Closing the Interview Strong

The final moments of an interview can have a significant impact on the interviewer's overall impression of you. This chapter will provide you with tips on how to wrap up the interview and express your genuine interest in the position effectively.

Reaffirm Your Interest

As the interview draws to a close, take the opportunity to reaffirm your enthusiasm and interest in the role. This can be done in a few ways:

1. **Direct Statement:** Clearly state your interest in the position and your desire to be part of the team. For example, "I am very excited about this opportunity and would be thrilled to join your team."

2. **Reiterate Your Qualifications:** Summarize how your skills and experiences make you the ideal candidate for the role. Highlight the keyways you can contribute to the company's success.

3. **Ask for the Job:** Consider taking a bold approach and directly asking for the position. This shows your confidence and commitment. You could say, "Based on our discussion, I believe I am the right person for this role, and I would love the chance to join your team."

Ask Insightful Questions

The end of the interview is also an excellent time to ask any remaining questions you have about the role, the company, or the next steps in the hiring process. Asking thoughtful questions shows your genuine interest and helps you gather information to figure out if the position is the right fit for you.

Some examples of strong closing questions include:

- "What are the next steps in the hiring process, and when should I expect to hear back from you?"
- "Is there any other information I can provide to help you make your decision?"
- "What are the key challenges someone in this role would face, and how would you envision me addressing them?"

Maintain Positive Body Language

Throughout the closing moments of the interview, continue to show positive body language. Maintain eye contact, sit up straight, and avoid crossed arms or legs. These nonverbal cues will reinforce your interest and enthusiasm.

Thank the Interviewer

As you wrap up the interview, be sure to thank the interviewer for their time and consideration. Express your appreciation for the opportunity to discuss the role and your qualifications.

Follow Up Promptly

After the interview, follow up with a thank-you note or email. This is an opportunity to reiterate your interest, highlight any key points you may have forgotten to mention, and provide any other information the interviewer asked.

Putting It All Together

By following these tips, you can close the interview on a strong note and leave a lasting positive impression on the interviewer. Demonstrating your enthusiasm, asking insightful questions, and following up effectively can set you apart from other candidates

D Helps
and increase your chances of moving forward in the hiring process.

Remember, the last moments of the interview are just as important as the rest. Approach the closing with the same level of preparation and professionalism to ensure you end the conversation on a high note.

Chapter 5: The Secrets to Success

The Art of the Thank-You Note

A well-crafted thank-you note can leave an impression on the interviewer and set you apart from other candidates. It's a chance to reiterate your interest in the position, highlight your qualifications, and show appreciation for the interviewer's time. Here's how to write a compelling thank-you note:

Why a Thank-You Note Matters

1. **Demonstrates Appreciation**: A thank-you note shows that you value the interviewer's time and consideration.

2. **Reiterates Interest:** It reinforces your enthusiasm for the position and the company.

3. **Provides Additional Information:** You can use the note to mention any important points you forgot to discuss during the interview.

4. **Sets You Apart:** A well-written thank-you note can differentiate you from other candidates and make you more memorable.

Tips for Writing a Compelling Thank-You Note

Here are some tips to help you write a compelling thank-you note:

1. **Be Prompt:** Send the note within 24 hours of the interview. This shows that you are enthusiastic about the opportunity and helps keep you top of mind for the interviewer.

2. **Be Sincere:** Express your genuine gratitude for the interviewer's time and consideration. Avoid generic phrases and be specific about what you appreciate about the conversation.

3. **Reiterate Interest:** Use the note to reiterate your interest in the position and the company. This helps to reinforce your enthusiasm and shows that you are serious about the opportunity.

4. **Personalize the Note:** Address the interviewer by name and reference specific points from the conversation. This shows that you were actively listening and helps to build a connection.
5. **Keep it Brief:** Aim for a length of around 100-150 words. Any longer and the note may start to feel too formal or insincere.
6. **Proofread:** Make sure to proofread the note carefully to ensure that it is free of errors and flows smoothly.
7. **Use a Professional Tone:** Use a professional tone and avoid using slang or overly casual language.

Example of a Compelling Thank-You Note
Here is an example of a compelling thank-you note:
Dear [Interviewer's Name],
I wanted to take a moment to express my sincere gratitude for the opportunity to interview for the [Position] role at [Company]. I truly appreciated the time you took to speak with me and share your insights about the company and the position.
After our conversation, I am even more confident that this is a company I would be proud to work for and contribute to. I am excited about the opportunity to bring my skills and experience to the team and help drive success.
Once again, thank you for your time and consideration. I look forward to the opportunity to discuss my qualifications further.
Best regards, [Your Name]

Putting It All Together
By following these tips, you can write a compelling thank-you note that helps to set you apart from other candidates and leaves a lasting impression on the interviewer. Remember to be prompt, sincere, and personalized in your note, and to reiterate your interest in the position and the company.

Following Up Effectively

Following up after an interview is a crucial step in the job search process. It shows initiative, interest in the position, and a willingness to take the next step. However, it's essential to follow up effectively without being overbearing or annoying the interviewer. Here are some strategies to help you follow up effectively:

Why Follow Up?

1. **Demonstrates Interest**: Following up shows that you are genuinely interested in the position and the company.

2. **Keeps You Top of Mind:** A follow-up can help keep you top of mind for the interviewer, especially if they are considering multiple candidates.

3. **Provides Additional Information**: A follow-up can offer an opportunity to share more information that may not have been discussed during the interview.

Strategies for Following Up

1. **Wait a Week**: Wait at least a week after the interview before following up. This allows the interviewer time to review your application and discuss your candidacy with other team members.

2. **Send a Thank-You Note:** Send a thank-you note or email to express your gratitude for the interviewer's time and reiterate your interest in the position.

3. **Make a Phone Call:** If you haven't heard back after a week, consider making a phone call to the interviewer. Keep the call brief and to the point and avoid being pushy or aggressive.

4. **Send a Follow-Up Email:** If you haven't heard back after a phone call, consider sending a follow-up email. Keep the email brief and to the point and avoid repeating information that has already been discussed.

Tips for Following Up Effectively

1. **Be Polite and Professional**: Always be polite and professional in your follow-up communication. Avoid

being pushy or aggressive, and never use a confrontational tone.

2. **Keep it Brief:** Keep your follow-up communication brief and to the point. Avoid repeating information that has already been discussed and focus on providing more information or reiterating your interest in the position.

3. **Don't Overdo It:** Don't overdo it with your follow-up communication. One or two follow-ups are sufficient, and any more than that can be seen as overbearing or annoying.

4. **Respect the Interviewer's Time:** Respect the interviewer's time and avoid following up too often. Give them time to review your application and discuss your candidacy with other team members.

Example of a Follow-Up Email

Here is an example of a follow-up email:

Subject: Following up on our interview

Dear [Interviewer's Name],

I hope this email finds you well. I wanted to follow up on our interview last week and express my continued interest in the [Position] role at [Company]. I truly appreciated the time you took to speak with me and share your insights about the company and the position.

I understand that hiring processes can take time, and I want to reiterate my enthusiasm for the opportunity to join your team. If there is any other information I can provide or if you would like to schedule a follow-up conversation, please let me know.

Thank you again for your time and consideration. I look forward to the opportunity to discuss my qualifications further.

Best regards, [Your Name]

Putting It All Together

By following these strategies and tips, you can follow up effectively after an interview and show initiative and interest in the position. Remember to be polite and professional, keep it brief, and respect the interviewer's time.

Building Relationships After the Interview

Building relationships with your interviewers and potential colleagues can give you a significant advantage in the hiring process. These relationships can offer valuable insights into the company culture, help you stay informed about the hiring process, and potentially lead to future opportunities. Here are some strategies to help you build and keep these relationships:

Why Build Relationships?

1. **Stay Informed:** Building relationships can help you stay informed about the status of your application and any updates on the position.

2. **Gain Insights:** Relationships with insiders can provide you with valuable insights into the company culture, team dynamics, and the interviewer's expectations.

3. **Networking Opportunities:** Building relationships can expand your professional network, opening the door to future opportunities even if you don't get the current job.

Strategies for Building Relationships

1. **Send a Thank-You Note:** After the interview, send a thank-you note to express your gratitude for the opportunity. Personalize the note by mentioning specific points from the interview and reiterating your interest in the position.

2. **Connect on LinkedIn:** Send a connection request to the interviewer or potential colleagues on LinkedIn. Include a

brief message reminding them of your interview and expressing your interest in staying connected.

3. **Follow Up Regularly:** Periodically check in with the interviewer to inquire about the status of your application. Be polite and respectful of their time and avoid being overbearing.

4. **Share Relevant Content:** Share articles, reports, or industry news that you think might be of interest to the interviewer. This shows that you are proactive and engaged in the field.

5. **Attend Company Events:** If the company hosts events, webinars, or networking sessions, attend these to build a stronger connection with the team.

6. **Offer Help:** If you have expertise in an area that could help the company, offer to help or share resources. This shows your willingness to contribute and be a team player.

Tips for Maintaining Relationships

1. **Be Genuine:** Authenticity is key in building relationships. Be genuine in your interactions and show a genuine interest in the other person.

2. **Listen Actively:** Pay attention to what the other person is saying and respond thoughtfully. This shows that you value their insights and opinions.

3. **Follow Through:** If you promise to send more information or follow up on a specific topic, make sure to do so promptly. This builds trust and credibility.

4. **Stay Positive:** Keep a positive attitude in your communications. Even if you don't get the job, staying positive can leave a good impression and open doors for future opportunities.

5. **Respect Boundaries:** Be mindful of the interviewer's time and respect their boundaries. Avoid over-communicating or being too persistent.

Conclusion

Building and keeping relationships after the interview can significantly enhance your chances of securing the job and expanding your professional network. By following these strategies and tips, you can create lasting connections that may lead to future opportunities.

Chapter 6: The Negotiation Process

Understanding Your Worth

Understanding your worth is crucial to negotiating a fair salary and benefits package. This chapter provides tips for evaluating your skills and experiences and figuring out your market value. It's helpful to have three numbers in mind: the dream number, the desired number, and the must-have number.

Negotiating Salary and Benefits

Negotiating salary and benefits can be challenging but is an essential part of the hiring process. Learn strategies for negotiating a fair compensation package that meets your needs. There may not be a lot of wiggle room. There is always another candidate. It may be that it isn't the position for you at this point in your career. Typically, the employer has a range based on experience, training and their current workforce skills. The greatest advantage of collaborating with recruiters and headhunters is that they know what the position will pay and if you're upfront with them they can help in this process. Playing two companies offers against each other rarely ever works. They need you or they don't. Look at the pros and cons of the deals and decide what position best fits your goals.

The Art of Compromise in Job Negotiations

Compromise is indeed a crucial part of the negotiation process, especially when it comes to job offers. It's about finding a middle ground that satisfies both parties without sacrificing your core goals or values. Let's dive into how you can master this art:

Understanding the Importance of Compromise

First off, it's important to understand why compromise matters. In negotiations, if you stick rigidly to your position, you might end up with nothing. On the other side, if you're too quick to give in, you might shortchange yourself. The sweet spot is somewhere in the middle.

Know Your Non-Negotiables

Before you even start negotiating, figure out what's absolutely essential for you. Is it the salary? The ability to work remotely? Career growth opportunities? Knowing your "must-haves" helps you find where you can be flexible.

Be Prepared to Give and Take

Negotiation is a two-way street. If you're asking for a higher salary, be prepared to take on additional responsibilities. If you want more vacation days, maybe you can be flexible on start date. It's all about balance.

Use the "If-Then" Approach

This is a great technique for finding compromise. For example, "If you can meet my salary requirements, then I'd be willing to start two weeks earlier than initially planned." This shows you're willing to be flexible while still advocating for your needs.

Listen Actively

Sometimes, the best compromises come from really understanding what the other party needs. Listen carefully to what the employer is saying - and what they're not saying. There might be constraints or concerns you haven't considered.

Think Creatively

Don't get stuck on the obvious negotiation points. Sometimes, thinking outside the box can lead to win-win solutions. Maybe they can't meet your salary requirements right now, but they could offer performance-based bonuses or additional training opportunities.

Maintain Professionalism

Even if things get tense, always keep your cool. Emotional outbursts or ultimatums rarely lead to good outcomes. Stay calm, polite, and professional throughout the process.

D Helps
Know When to Walk Away

While compromise is important, there's a line between compromise and settling. If the offer doesn't meet your core needs and you've exhausted all avenues for negotiation, it's okay to walk away. There might be better opportunities out there.

Practice Makes Perfect

Like any skill, negotiation and compromise get easier with practice. Role-play with a friend or mentor before your actual negotiation. This can help you feel more comfortable and prepared.

Remember, at the end of the day, both you and the employer want the same thing - for you to join the team and contribute to the company's success. Approach compromise with this mindset, and you're more likely to find a solution that works for everyone.

So, next time you're in a negotiation, take a deep breath, know your worth, but also be open to finding that middle ground. That's the art of compromise and mastering it can open doors to amazing opportunities.

Chapter 7: Common Interview Mistakes to Avoid

Overcoming Interview Anxiety

Interview anxiety is a common challenge for many job seekers. Here are strategies to help you manage and overcome interview anxiety:

- **Prepare Thoroughly:** One of the main causes of anxiety is the fear of the unknown. Prepare extensively by researching the company, practicing common interview questions, and rehearsing your responses.

- **Visualize Success:** Imagine yourself acing the interview and getting the job. Positive visualization can help boost your confidence and reduce anxiety.

- **Breathing Exercises:** Deep breathing can help calm your nerves. Take a few deep breaths before the interview to relax.

- **Arrive Early:** Get to the interview location early. This gives you time to collect your thoughts and compose yourself before the interview.

- **Stay Hydrated:** Make sure you drink plenty of water before and during the interview. Dehydration can worsen anxiety.

The Importance of a Positive Attitude

A positive attitude can make a significant difference in your interview performance. Here's how to maintain a positive outlook:

- **Focus on Your Strengths:** Instead of worrying about your weaknesses, focus on your strengths and the skills that make you a strong candidate.

- **Stay Positive:** Keep a positive mindset by reminding yourself of your achievements and why you are a good fit for the role.

D Helps
- **Practice Positive Self-Talk:** Encourage yourself with positive affirmations. This can help you stay confident and motivated.

- **Learn from Rejections:** If you have been rejected before, use those experiences as learning opportunities. Analyze what went wrong and how you can improve for the next interview.

Chapter 8: Advanced Interview Techniques

Behavioral Interviewing: A Deep Dive

Behavioral interviewing is a popular technique used by many employers. This chapter provides an in-depth look at behavioral interviewing and offers strategies for answering behavioral questions effectively.

- **Understanding Behavioral Interviewing:** Behavioral interviewing focuses on questions that require candidates to describe specific situations they have encountered and how they managed them.

- **Example:** "Tell me about a time when you failed."

The STAR Method: A Framework for Effective Storytelling

The STAR method (Situation, Task, Action, Result) is a powerful tool for structuring your answers to behavioral interview questions. Learn how to use this framework to tell compelling stories about your experiences

STAR Method:

- **Situation:** Describe the specific situation or challenge you faced.

- **Task:** Explain the task or goal you were trying to achieve.

- **Action:** Detail the steps you took to address the situation or task.

- **Result:** Highlight the outcome of your actions and the positive impact you made.

Case Interview Strategies

Case interviews are commonly used in industries like consulting and finance. Here are strategies for preparing for and acing case interviews:

D Helps

- **Understand the Case Format:** Case interviews typically involve presenting a business problem or scenario and asking the candidate to analyze it and propose a solution.

- **Practice with Sample Cases:** Prepare by practicing with sample cases available online or through case interview books.

- **Develop a Structured Approach:** Use frameworks like the 3Cs (Client, Company, Competitors) or the MECE (Mutually Exclusive, Collectively Exhaustive) principle to structure your analysis.

- **Communicate Clearly:** Present your analysis clearly and concisely, highlighting key points and recommendations.

Group Interview Tips

Group interviews can be challenging but also offer unique opportunities to showcase your skills and abilities. Here are tips for standing out in a group interview setting:

- **Be Prepared to Introduce Yourself:** Be ready to give a brief introduction that highlights your relevant skills and experiences.

- **Participate Actively:** Engage in discussions and contribute your thoughts and ideas. However, avoid dominating the conversation.

- **Listen Carefully:** Pay attention to what others are saying and respond thoughtfully.

Chapter 9: Exceptional Answers to Common Interview Questions

Top Interview Questions

Here are some top interview questions along with tips on how to answer them effectively:

- **Tell Me About Yourself:** Keep your answer concise and focused on your professional background and relevant skills. Example: "I'm an initiative-taking and purposeful professional with a passion for [industry/field]. I have [number] years of experience in [relevant skills]."

- **Why Are You Interested in This Position?** Show that you've done your research on the company and explain how your skills align with the role. Example: "I'm drawn to this position because it aligns perfectly with my career goals and allows me to leverage my strengths in [specific skills]."

- **What Are Your Strengths and Weaknesses?** Be honest about your weaknesses but frame them as areas for improvement. Highlight your strengths and provide examples. Example: "One of my strengths is my diligence. One area I'm working on is improving my public speaking skills."

Behavioral Interview Questions

Here are some behavioral interview questions along with tips on how to answer them using the STAR method:

- **Tell Me About a Time When You Failed:** Use the STAR method to describe the situation, task, actions, and result.

    - **S - Situation:** In my previous role as a project manager at a software development company, our team was tasked with launching a new mobile application for a major retail client. The deadline was tight, and expectations were high.

- **T - Task:** My responsibility was to ensure that all aspects of the project, from design to deployment, were completed on time and met the client's requirements. This included coordinating with various teams such as developers, designers, and quality assurance specialists.

- **A - Action:** I decided to rely heavily on a new project management tool that promised to streamline our workflow. However, I underestimated the learning curve for the team and did not give enough time for training and adaptation. Additionally, I did not conduct frequent enough check-ins with team members to address any issues early on.

- **R - Result:** Due to unfamiliarity with the new tool and the lack of prompt communication, there were significant delays and miscommunications within the team. We missed the initial launch deadline, which led to client dissatisfaction and additional stress on the team.

- **What I learned from this experience:** This failure taught me several valuable lessons. First, I realized the importance of thoroughly evaluating new tools and technologies before implementing them. Second, I learned that clear, frequent communication is crucial for keeping a project on track. Lastly, I understood that even with tight deadlines, giving time for training and adaptation is essential for the success of the project.

- **Since this experience, I have made it a point to conduct thorough assessments before introducing new tools and to keep regular check-ins with my team to ensure everyone is aligned and any issues are addressed promptly.

Technical Interview Questions

Here are some technical interview questions along with tips on how to answer them effectively:

- **What Is Your Experience with [Specific Skill or Technology]?** Give specific examples of your experience and how it applies to the role. Example: "I have [number] years of experience working with [specific skill or technology]. I've used it to [specific project or task] and achieved [specific result]."

Situational Interview Questions

Here are some situational interview questions along with tips on how to answer them effectively:

- **How Would You Manage a Situation Where a Coworker Is Consistently Late to Meetings?** Describe a structured approach to addressing the issue. Example: "First, I would try to understand the reason for their lateness. If it's a recurring issue, I'd have a private conversation to discuss the impact on the team and offer solutions. If the problem persists, I'd escalate the issue to a supervisor."

General Interview Questions

Here are some general interview questions along with tips on how to answer them effectively:

- **What Are Your Salary Expectations?** Be open but also strategic. Research the market value and be prepared to negotiate. Example: "I'm open to discussing compensation based on the specific role and responsibilities. I'm more interested in finding a position that aligns with my career goals and offers opportunities for growth."

Chapter 10: Questions You Should Ask

Why Asking Questions is Crucial

Asking questions during an interview is not just about gathering information; it also proves your genuine interest in the role and the company. Here are some guidelines for asking meaningful questions:

- **Avoid Easily Answered Questions:** Avoid asking questions that can be easily answered by researching the company online. Instead, focus on questions that require insight from the interviewer and show that you have done your homework.

- **Tailoring Your Questions:** Ensure your questions are relevant and insightful by tailoring them to the specific role and company.

Examples of questions you can ask:

- **Company Culture and Values:** "How would you describe the company culture and what type of employee tends to thrive here?"

- **Professional Development:** "How does the company approach professional development and continuous learning for its employees?"

- **Team Dynamics:** "Can you tell me about the team I'll be working with and how collaboration is encouraged?"

A Personal Anecdote: The Importance of Fit

Here's an illustrative story that highlights the importance of asking the right questions to ensure the role is a good fit:

- **An applicant once took a CFO position in Fort Worth, moving his family from Seattle. His son was in his senior year of high school, and after a long job search, this position seemed like a dream come true. However,** three months into the job, they parted ways due to a mismatch in company culture. Asking the right questions can help you avoid such mismatches.

Ensuring the Right Fit

When asking questions, keep in mind what is important to you in a role. Here are some added questions that can help you figure out if the role is a good fit:

- **Daily Responsibilities:** "Could you elaborate on the day-to-day responsibilities of this role?"

- **Success Metrics:** "How do you measure success in this role?"

- **Personal Enjoyment:** "What do you enjoy most about working here?"

- **Future Initiatives:** "What's one exciting thing going on at your company right now?"

I have spoken about using your questions throughout your interview. Again, prepare a list that highlights aspects of the position that you are curious about and that could uncover insights that may be used to set you apar from other applicants. By asking these questions, you not only prove your interest but also gather valuable information that can help you decide if the role aligns with your goals and values.

D Helps

Chapter 11: Professionalism in the Interview

The Importance of Maintaining Professionalism

Professionalism is crucial throughout the entire interview process. Here are some key points to consider:

- **Always Maintain Professionalism:** Even if you feel comfortable after spending time with the employer, never let your guard down.

- **Avoid Personal Comments:** Steer clear of personal remarks or jokes, especially those involving appearance or family members.

- **Focus on Your Qualifications:** Employers want to know what your experiences and training can do for their company or department.

Case Study: A Professionalism Misstep

Consider the following true scenario:

- **A candidate, after his third interview, spent the day with the company president as the final decision on a role. Toward the end of the day, sitting in the president's office, the candidate made a joke in relation to how beautiful the president's wife was, as he was commenting on the president's family picture proudly displayed on the desk. This comment led to the deal falling through.**

Virtual Interview Tips

For virtual interviews, professionalism extends to your environment and presentation:

- **Environment:** Ensure your background is professional and free from distractions.

- **Audio Quality:** Make sure there are no disruptive noises, like a barking dog.
- **Lighting:** Ensure your space is well-lit so you're clearly visible.
- **Professional Attire:** Dress appropriately, as you would for an in-person interview.

Practical Tips for Maintaining Professionalism

Here are some practical tips to keep professionalism during the interview:

1. **Be Prepared:** Research the company and the role thoroughly. Know how to articulate your experiences and skills in a way that aligns with the company's values and goals.
2. **Maintain Eye Contact:** Whether in person or on video, keeping eye contact shows confidence and engagement.
3. **Clear Communication:** Speak clearly and concisely. Avoid using slang or making inappropriate jokes.
4. **Follow-Up:** After the interview, send a thank-you note to express your appreciation and reiterate your interest in the role.

Chapter 12: The Close

How to Express Your Interest in the Job

Expressing your interest in the job can leave an impression on the interviewer. Here's how to communicate your enthusiasm effectively:

- **Be Direct:** Look the interviewer in the eye and say something like:
    - "I'd love to be part of your team."
    - "After our discussion, I'm even more excited about this opportunity and would be thrilled to join your organization."
    - "I feel like I would be a great fit for this role and your company culture."
- **Ask for the Position:** One particularly bold candidate even said, "It's okay for you to hire me." While this level of directness might not be right in all situations, it certainly made an impression.

The Power of Asking for the Position

Want to really stand out? Ask for the position outright. Tell them you want to be there. This shows confidence, enthusiasm, and genuine interest—all qualities that employers value.

The Importance of Body Language

Your interest isn't just communicated through words. Employers notice your body language too:

- **Maintain Eye Contact:** Sitting on the edge of your chair, paying rapt attention to their questions—these nonverbal cues speak volumes about your engagement and interest.

What Not to Do

On the other side, here are some common mistakes to avoid:

- **Reading the Newspaper in the Lobby:** Avoid distractions like reading or using your phone before the interview.

- **Talking on the Phone:** Avoid talking on the phone before the interview.

- **Bringing Family Members:** Avoid bringing family members to the interview. (it happens)

Chapter 13: Follow-Up and Networking

Sending a Thank-You Note?

A well-crafted thank-you note can set you apart from other candidates. Here's how to write one:

- **Address the Interviewer:** Make sure to address the interviewer by name and reiterate your interest in the position.

- **Personalize:** Use the information gathered during the meeting to personalize your notes.

- **Send a Thank-You Note:** A well-crafted thank-you note can reinforce your interest and leave a positive impression.

Building Your Network

Building a strong professional network can open doors to new opportunities. Here are some strategies for building and keeping a robust network:

- **Attend Industry Events:** Attend conferences, seminars, and other industry events to meet people in your field. About this, when attending events, it's not your job to meet everyone in the room. Have a few meaningful conversations with the right people. I visited an HR gathering for senior and upcoming candidates. I was impressed with the event and made a few great connections. One eager jobseeker visited a few minutes and was impressive, right up to the moment I was told "I need to meet more people." Left me feeling our conversation was all about them not what we were looking for.

- **Use LinkedIn:** Leverage LinkedIn and other professional platforms to connect with professionals in your industry. I won't underestimate evening a post to Facebook to your

55

friends with your Hank Hill elevator pitch can uncover a connection.

- **Join Professional Organizations:** Joining professional organizations can provide opportunities to network and build relationships. You will get out what you put in. If you are active, you will find rewards.

Leveraging LinkedIn and Other Professional Platforms

LinkedIn and other professional platforms can be valuable tools for networking and job searching. Here's how to leverage them:

- **Complete Your Profile:** Ensure your profile is complete and up to date.
- **Engage with Content:** Engage with posts from others in your network to build relationships.
- **Reach Out to Connections:** Don't be afraid to reach out to connections for advice or to explore job opportunities.
- **Join me on LinkedIn Why? Headhunters have AWSOME NETWORKS.**
  http://www.linkedin.com/in/derekphelpsrecruiter

Chapter 14: Conclusion

D Helps
Recap of Key Takeaways

This chapter recaps the key takeaways from the guide, providing a summary of the most important strategies and tips for acing your next interview. **Recap of Key Takeaways**
As we conclude this comprehensive guide to acing your next interview, let's review the key takeaways:

- Preparation is key: Research the company, practice your responses, and prepare your materials.

- First impressions matter: Dress professionally, arrive early, and be confident.

- Show enthusiasm and interest: Ask questions, engage with the interviewer, and express your passion for the role.

- Highlight your strengths: Emphasize your skills, experience, and achievements.

- Learn from your mistakes: Use failures as opportunities to gain experience and improve.

Final Words of Encouragement

Finding the right job can be a challenging and often emotional journey, but with the right preparation and mindset, you can significantly increase your chances of success.

Stay Motivated

Staying positive and motivated is crucial throughout your job search. Here are some key strategies to help you keep your motivation:

- **Set Goals**: Break down your job search into manageable tasks and set small, achievable goals. This could include applying to a certain number of jobs per day, updating your social media profiles, or researching a specific number of companies per week.

- **Create a Routine**: Treat your job search like a full-time job. Establish a daily or weekly schedule that includes dedicated time for job searching, networking, and professional development. This routine will help you stay grounded and focused. You may need to remind your friends and loved ones you are finding a position. You are not available for the chores.

- **Build a Support Network**: Surround yourself with people who make you feel motivated to succeed. This could include friends, family, coworkers, or network connections. Regularly check in with your support network to share updates and seek encouragement. Create a board of directors that holds you accountable for your search activities.

Continuous Learning

Continuous learning is essential for professional growth. Here's how you can stay updated and focused:

- **Stay Updated with Industry Trends**: Keep abreast of the latest developments in your industry. This will not only make you a more attractive candidate but also help you stay motivated by seeing the opportunities and advancements in your field.

- **Read and Reflect**: Reading books related to your industry and career goals can provide valuable insights and inspiration. Reflecting on what you've read can help you align your goals and actions.

One dynamic speaker and trainer shared a short story with me years ago that helped shape some of this philosophy on getting out of the endless circle of poor finances and dead-end jobs. Realizing he had only a pocketful of change to buy lunch at the school where he coached, he knew he needed a change. Turning to his uncle, who was quite successful in life and finances, he sought guidance. His uncle asked three questions:

One, "Have you written your goals down?" His response was, "I have New Year's resolutions."

D Helps

Two, "Have you been to any training seminars or courses recently?" His response was, "Well, I have a Master's degree, but no, it's been years."

Three, "Have you read any good books lately?" The question left him digging through his mind. He was a teacher but couldn't remember his last book.

The uncle closed the door in his face and left him on the porch to ponder what had been asked. Ten years later, I visited his new palatial ranch only a few miles from the poor neighborhood where he grew up and taught. He handed me a copy of his latest book.

Managing Frustration and Discouragement

It's normal to feel overwhelmed, frustrated, or discouraged at times during your job search. Are you dreaming more? Have you found that you are declining activities that were enjoyable in the past? One story to share is from a 20-year veteran in the airline industry who said that being let go had a devastating impact on her finances. She shared that she had been in counseling for over 6 months. I urge you to use the tips in this chapter to care for yourself

Here are some tips to help you navigate these feelings:

- **Reframe Rejections**: View rejections as opportunities to learn and grow rather than as failures. Use feedback from employers to find areas for improvement and adjust your strategy accordingly.

- **Practice Self-Care**: Ensure you get plenty of rest, eat healthy meals, drink plenty of water, and incorporate exercise into your routine. Taking regular breaks and engaging in fun activities can help you recharge and support your mental and physical health.

Celebrate Small Wins

Staying motivated involves celebrating your small wins along the way. Here's how you can do this:

- **Acknowledge Your Efforts**: Count your daily activities as wins, no matter how small they may seem. This helps in maintaining a positive outlook and keeps you motivated.

- **Focus on Progress**: Celebrate the progress you make each day or week. Whether it's completing a certain number of applications or connecting with new people in your industry, acknowledging these achievements can boost your morale.

Seek Additional Resources

You are not alone on this journey. Here are some resources to help you stay motivated and informed:

- **YouTube and Social Media**: Reach out to us on YouTube at www.youtube.com/@derekphelps3715 or connect with us on Facebook at facebook.com/recruiterandheadhunter. We offer added videos, tips, and hacks to help in your job search journey.

- **Direct Support**: If you have any specific questions or need further assistance, feel free to reach out to your friendly headhunter at buildmybizz@gmail.com. Please take a moment if you found one actionable idea and share your review, we are here to help you navigate this process and land your dream job.

Finding the right job takes time and persistence. Remember that every "no" brings you closer to the "yes" you're looking for. Stay focused on your goals, celebrate your small wins, and take care of your mental and physical health.

"You are not alone." Together, we'll navigate this process, and with the right mindset and strategies, you'll be well on your way to landing your dream job. Keep pushing forward and remember that success often requires patience and determination. Your dream job is out there, and with persistence and the right support, you will find it.

D Helps
D Helps
Derek Phelps